LIELLE AMORÉT

I0518605

in the beginning,
love
found me

Copyright © 2025 Lielle Amorét

All rights reserved.

No part of this book may be reproduced, or stored in a retrieval system,

or transmitted in any form or by any means, electronic, mechanical,

photocopying, recording, or otherwise, without express written permission

of the publisher, except in the case of brief quotations

used in critical reviews or scholarly references.

First Edition

ISBN: 979-8-9923764-0-1

from the depths of my heart,

in hopes of reaching yours.

contents

prologue

I am led to introduce the God I know to the world.
I cannot introduce the God of Abraham or the God who
instructed Moses to lead His people out of slavery to you,
because I cannot relate to them. my unique creation, my
personalized crash-outs, introduced me to the God I know
now.

I was born into a Christian home, but let's be real, I had to
find my reason to serve Him. being a Christian just because
my parents are, is not sincere. if I want to believe in a
higher power, I shouldn't avoid the question: why do you
believe in God? depending on others' faith did nothing for
me. I wanted to see and witness Him for myself.

honestly, the only way I would believe, was if He suddenly
called my name in a deep, dramatic voice, or gave me a
jumpscare by appearing in front of me (the Old Testament
gave me wild ideas on encounters with God.) I had to learn
that seeing isn't believing and that faith without substance
is dead. but instead of building my faith, these doubts made
me feel condemned, unworthy to face Him.

the constant reinforcement of God's wrath only fueled my fear. the worldly view of God as judgmental, wrathful, and authoritarian had me questioning if He was indeed the righteous and just God they preached. to find God, I had to find myself, but I hated my reflection.

it wasn't until I gathered the courage to look in the mirror that I realized the God I desperately wanted to see was within me all along. it took a while, but I found the reason for my being. with that, I can introduce to you the One who made me believe:
He who loved me first.

aurora

dawn rises softly,
whispering to me,
you can begin again

from me,

you cannot give up. I see the depth of your pain, the countless tears you have shed, and the many attacks you have fought just to breathe. you've endured so much, and yet, you're still here. it breaks my heart to witness the words of insecure voices and envious gazes constantly scare a beautiful soul like yours. please remember, the most powerful and precious part of you is your capacity to love. it's good to love. don't let that love grow cold; the warmth of your heart and the light in your smile are rare gifts this world desperately needs.

I know it feels overwhelming, and you may be tempted to shut yourself off from the world, but genuineness is rare these days. you have encountered those who took your kindness for granted, who only sought to take without a need to give back. but others will appreciate you wholeheartedly. learn to discern who deserves a place in your heart. pain has been your teacher, but it was never meant to be your home. this pain has taught us that it's essential to ensure your cup is full before pouring it into someone else's. don't abandon the beauty of love. closing yourself off as a shield will only dim the light you were blessed with.

when you realize how vital that light is to
your existence, you may search for it again,
only to encounter the shadows of buried pains.
confronting these wounds can feel daunting,
but releasing trauma and unlearning old
coping mechanisms is part of your healing.
I don't wish for your journey to unfold in
despair. please permit yourself to let go and
feel. even in the darkest moments, there's
potential for growth and transformation. find
your way back to yourself, one step at a time,
even if it's just one tear. there's greater
love ahead, and He's patient, understanding,
and faithful. you were never alone, and He is
where your story truly begins.

to you

healing begins when hands let go
of what cannot be held,
and hearts open
to what remains within.

- for those ready to heal

for the weary,
for the hearts aching for change,

for those prepared
to face past mistakes,
to make peace with all they find,

for those who search
for the best within themselves,
even when it's hard to see.

for the ones that say they're healed
yet the heart still lingers in pain

come with an open heart,
and let us see
where this journey leads.

to you who carry unseen battles,
a darkness waiting to be met

know this, the courage to heal
is when we meet the parts of ourselves
we've long avoided.

our wounds run deep,
rooted in memories left unhealed.

don't grow numb to the calls of pain,
the voices of regret,
the moments left unfinished,

they don't call to punish,
but to be seen, to be named,
to be understood.

looking back and reflecting
isn't weakness, it's courage.
it's gathering pieces of love,
pain from repeated mistakes,
and holding them in trembling hands.

not to forget, but to forgive,
not to erase, but to make peace.
the past is a teacher that tells,
you're more than what has hurt you,
and more substantial
than what has tried to ruin you.

healing starts when you stop searching
everywhere else,
and finally look within.
it's when exhaustion wraps around you
like a heavy cloak.
then, you're tired
of the life you're living,
tired of nothing working out,
tired of daydreaming about the person
you wish you could be.

the first step? acknowledge it.
acknowledge the pain, the missteps,
the moments you silenced your gut
when it screamed for your attention,
and the ways you've hurt others
just as they've hurt you.

healing isn't about pretending
to be strong; it's about admitting
you're not strong enough
to carry it alone.
in that admission, strength is restored,
and we're ready to rebuild.

it's never a straight path,
it's a messy journey,
waltz of forward steps and stumbles,
where each setback reminds us that
even detours shape the destination.

within each heart lies
the capacity to heal, grow,
to untangle the threads of our past,
and find our way home to ourselves.

to heal, I began with forgiveness,
a lesson learned in the pits of regret.
I faced how I settled for less,
untangling the shame
of withholding love from my soul.

for every drop poured into those
who left me empty,
my worth lay hidden.
I forgave the shallow need
to find love in others' hands,
to chase affection as an aid,
when love was meant to dwell
first within my heart.

most of all, I forgave myself
for turning away from God,
the One who never turned from me,
the One who cradled the faith
I couldn't hold,
believed when I was entangled
with depression, and stayed
when I couldn't see.

I found Him after I forgave myself.
yet, He was there the whole time,
waiting with open arms, as if to say,
"thank you for finally noticing Me."

strength comes from God,
so there's no need
to shy away from weakness.
a pretentious life is meaningless,
and every heart has its breaking point.

bottling up pain
is like sealing a jar too tightly.
the pressure builds
until it shatters in your hands.
only He knows how to handle,
to twist it open, release the weight,
and let it breathe.

that's His role in healing,
carrying the load
so you can keep walking.
numbness can't give relief
to a place that is meant to feel.

raw pain creates the best form of art,
for within pain lies love.
to create from pain is to offer
a piece of yourself to the world,
to give the ache meaning.
to show that even a flower
can bloom in withering soil,
proving that beauty
isn't bound by circumstance,
but by resilience.

within every scar,
a story of love remains,
reminding us
that nothing is ever truly lost,
when it's shared.

to create is not only to make,
but to become.
each thought, each word,
a small piece of becoming.

       - you are a creator

there's a truth
crafted into the beginning,
an indication of who we are:
inherently creative,
formed by the same breath
that spoke life into all things.

this is our foundation,
to know ourselves,
to embrace the power within.
let this be the beginning
where we embody that truth.

we're simply actors,
our minds, the scriptwriters.
as it's in your mind,
so it will be in your life.

everything we need to be fulfilled
lives within us.
that's why God spoke to us,
"be fruitful and multiply."
for we hold the power
to bring life into all we envision.

we're creators,
breathing reality into existence
by simply being.

our words hold the fate
of life and death.
our words can breathe life into dreams,
or extinguish them
beneath shadows of doubt.

the initial step is a thought.
with intention, it begins to exist.

our minds are gardens,
each thought a seed,
waiting to bloom into reality.

thinking alone isn't enough,
it's just the start.
we must nourish our thoughts
with purpose, watering them
with belief and determination.

to control my thoughts,
I hand my doubts to God,
embracing those that illuminate my path.
I trust His light to guide me,
bringing clarity and vision
with every step.

I can speak of my God with you,
but the most authentic revelation
of His nature
is your relationship with Him.
you'll find His fingerprints
embedded in your soul
when you discover who you are.

discipline is the quiet force
that carries you from who you are,
to who you're meant to be.
growth demands it,
and change waits for it.

- stand on discipline

discipline isn't easy.
it's showing up
when you don't feel like it,
doing what needs to be done,
even when no one is watching.

if you want to change your life,
stop lying to yourself,
making excuses,
and waiting for motivation.

it's not about perfection;
it's about consistency.
it's deciding every day
that you're worth the effort.

self-sabotage is a loop,
playing on repeat until it's broken.
it hides behind comfort,
disguised as fear or doubt,
pretending to protect,
but it keeps things small.

the walls weren't raised by chance;
they're made of repeated choices.
as long as the same habits persist,
nothing will change.

growth requires stepping out of
patterns that keep you stagnant,
unlearning the traumas,
and making room for the person
you were destined to become.

stop asking if it works.
stop waiting for someone else's proof.
the only way to know
is to do **it** yourself.

we camp on the sidelines,
scrolling through comments,
looking for reassurance,
waiting for another to validate what
we should be experiencing firsthand.
whether it's a workout, new habits,
a business, or self-care routines—
it w**ork**s when you work towards it.

results don't come from watching
or wondering, they come from action.
so stop asking and start moving.
do it, stay consistent,
and let your own results be the answer.

just say no
to the invitations that steal your time,
to the expectations of a world
that doesn't understand your vision.

just say no, because "no."
is a complete sentence.
it's a boundary drawn,
the power to choose what builds you
over what breaks you.

just say no to friends who call
but don't listen, and to plans
that drain but don't pour.
sometimes, the path forward
requires stepping away.

just say no,
because isolation isn't loneliness,
but a place of revelation.
when the noise fades,
you'll hear the voices
that remind you of who you are.

don't settle for less,
when a King stepped down from glory,
bearing the weight of the world
to crown you with salvation.

don't settle for half-hearted love.
no jewelry, no bare minimum,
can match the priceless gift
of your peace and well-being.

don't settle for a life
that leaves you longing.
you're made for abundance,
to thrive, not just to survive.
anything less denies the truth
of who you are.

don't see discipline
as the bridge between who you are
and who you wish to become.
you're already that person.

discipline is merely the hand
that guides you into alignment,
bringing the present you in step
with the values of your perfected self.

if you believe discipline
is something you must acquire
to be successful,
you'll remain trapped in hesitation,
waiting for worthiness to arrive.

but if you know success
is your birthright,
then success will move through you,
and everything within and around you
will shift to match that truth.

the body is an echo of the mind,
a receiver of the commands we give it.
speak life into your being,
and your body will vibrate
with the frequency of wealth,
of peace, of joy
of the fruitfulness
already written into you
as an inheritor of the Kingdom of God.

dear reader,

there are many ways we learn to guard love,
chase it, or question if it was ever real.
maybe you loved loud
or maybe you ghosted and called it pride.

maybe you shut down or opened too quickly
or felt too much
or not enough.

maybe you don't know what love feels like
unless it hurts a little.
or maybe you only recognize it in silence.

there is no shame
in the way you've learned to love.
this is a return away from who the world
taught you to be, and to the one God always
saw, when He called you very good.
love has never stopped looking for you
and neither has He.

from the soil of love
I bloom,
rooted in their embrace

before creation, there was love.
with love,
God spoke light into darkness,
and from nothing, He shaped everything.

He crafted the earth with His wisdom:
the skies, stars, oceans, and land.
He saw that it was good,
but His masterpiece was perfected
when He made us.

from the sands of the earth,
in His image, He breathed life
into our lungs, filling us with joy,
with peace,
and ultimately, love.

love is the very essence of who God is.
the heartbeat of the universe,
the driving force behind every creation.

how you love
reveals the depth of your soul,
and your way of living
is a mirror to the love you give.

love is the wisdom God speaks,
and we're meant to reflect it
in everything we do.

we were created in the image of love.
love found us first,
before we knew its name,
before we understood its power.

love existed as a truth to be embraced.
we were already loved,
fully, completely, divinely.

before I had a name, Love knew me.
before I ever reached for Love,
Love knitted me
in the comfort of His mercy.
I wasn't an accident.
not a variable that needed a why
to define my value.
I was spoken into existence
by a Love that didn't hesitate.

the world didn't teach me love;
Love taught the world about me.
long before I asked for proof,
before I knew what it meant
to be chosen, I was already favored
in the arms of eternity.

before I ever loved Him,
He loved me first.

lielle

of hebrew origin, meaning "God is mine."
gifted to the hands that shaped my
beginning, revealed to earth on the eve of
spring's awakening, in the year of
the dragon.

one pair of brown eyes.

they say the eyes are windows to the soul,
and hers, warm and brown, carry a light that
incites the world to linger. an intuitive
heart, a reflective mind, an artist whose
spirit paints silently. she is a mosaic of
mysteries, understood only by those who look
with care. her gaze reaches beyond what is
seen, uncovering truths within one's spirit.
in her eyes that love blooms, she invites
others to find love in all they do. to see
beauty where it once was hidden, to cherish
the overlooked and the small, to embrace
each unique design. for in all things,
beauty waits, a masterpiece, waiting to be
appreciated.

a bowl full of glowing melanated skin.

rich as chocolate, sweetened with golden
honey, this is both her shield and her
crown. in a world where her skin sparks
controversy, her melanin shields her from
the sun's fierce rays and defies the weight
of adversity. thick-skinned, she stands
strong, yet even resilience craves warmth.
wrap her in kindness, for the beauty of
Lielle lies not in her skin, but within the
depths of her heart.

a deep voice crafted in the wells of wisdom.

a gift once misused, letting harsh words
escape, though harm was never her intention.
her voice had often been silenced, drowned
out by the noise of others, misunderstood in
its gentleness. her voice is now aligned
with that frequency, letting love shape
every utterance. she speaks not to fill the
air, but to plant seeds in fertile minds. an
observer by nature, studying the world
before offering her truth. not every ear is
attuned to wisdom, and she refuses to waste
words on those unwilling to hear. her voice
craves meaning, a dive into what life truly
means, the energy behind every word, the
mystery beneath each moment. through her
sound, she hopes to awaken others, to spark
a light that leads them inward, to something
greater, to something divine.

love was my first teacher.
it began with my mother's embrace,
my grandfather's warmth,
a love that adored me,
as if I were the center of their world.

I imagine it like a child's affection
for sparkly bubbles,
mesmerized by the magic
that keeps the pretty ball afloat.
a love that engraved into my soul:
you matter.

love also left me confused.
my parents' dynamic was nothing
like the fairytales I read.
their love looked like struggle,
like suffocation,
like a bond that kept them together
even when it hurts.
it made me wonder,
what is love?

I was the trail run, the first attempt
at love and responsibility.
under their watchful eyes,
I stumbled,
felt the hold of their expectations
press me down.
mistakes became lessons,
each one carving its scar.

still, I survived.
in surviving, I grew stronger,
for myself and those who come after me,
the ones who would follow
in the path I paved.

the first of six,
the first to ever do it.
the first to cry,
the first to laugh,
the first to feel
the affection of Grandpa's hands.

the first to witness love,
a love that began with two,
then grew to three, and now more.
the first to say mom and dad
to two hearts
that never heard of it before.

a heavy title,
a burden too great.
the first grandchild,
the firstborn daughter,
bound by a duty to stand strong,
deemed weak if she admits
that she's scared.

the first to fall,
the first to crack,
because breaking the first
creates a track.

the first must be steel
to hold the rest,
to shield them from trials,
to pass each test.
the first to see love's heartbreak
and loss, to learn the world's truths
at any cost.
the first to know
that love is a seed,
but not all will grow.

born to lead, to hold the line,
to be the anchor when the storm arrives.
with every step is a fear she hides.
that if she falters,
the family will fall.

firstborn daughters,
we are made to succeed,
but this success doesn't come freely.
seasons of sorrow, seasons of doubt,
feeling unworthy
but never speaking out.

with the burden of the family's honor,
her shoulders bend,
the traumas she's seen,
she must defend.

I yearned for control,
to shield myself from the unknown.
I thought control was sanity,
a way to keep chaos from my throne.

I wrapped my fear in strict rules,
forged in the path of my upbringing,
set by hands that grew gentle
for the ones who came after me.

I clung to control,
and found it hard to obey.

I cared for the younger,
sacrificed my youth to give them peace.
I was met with nothing but,
"you're so mature for your age."
as if I had chosen this.

they have me to look up to,
to show them the way,
but who do I turn to
when the night dominates the day?

I wear the mantle of a mother's heart,
cold as the one
I swore I wouldn't imitate.
I may look like them,
but I'm not the same.

we carry the same last name,
but I'll carve my lane.
proud to be the pillar,
unyielding and alone,
I helped raise them,
so this throne is mine to own.

we look to our parents
to teach us what love means,
how to feel safe, how to trust,
how to be cherished.

but not all children
are met with kindness.
some grow in homes where love is scarce,
where affection is a foreigner,
and traumas carve deep.

for those children,
parental love becomes a tangled web,
a quilt with threads of confusion,
of moments that hurt.

in homes where love is absent,
children learn to guard their hearts,
to question their worth,
to seek validation
in places that will never satisfy.

they are taught
that love can be conditional,
that it can be withheld,
that it can feel more like a shadow
than a warm embrace.

and so they grow,
with a distorted understanding of love.
a love tied to pain and disappointment,
that demands but rarely gives.

even in despair, hope lingers.
for love is resilient,
waiting to be found
beyond the walls of childhood.

those who have known the absence of love
can still learn to love
in the truest sense,
can still find strength to heal,
to open their hearts to the love
they were always meant to know.

through understanding,
they reclaim love as their own,
redefining what it means
to love and be loved.

my mother's hands never knew rest,
shaped by a place
where love was left unsaid.
in the palm of her hands
a promise was traced,
a family of purpose,
one she would create.

her touch defied the past she knew,
loving through absence,
pouring from what was empty,
believing if she gave enough,
enough might return.

a mother's heart stretched far and wide,
an open door, a haven of grace,
for all who seek her boundless embrace.

in the depths of her sorrow she guards.
an angel with hidden wings,
carrying the agonies of our sufferings,
allowing them to flow
through her prayers.

we're drawn to the beauty of her smile,
like butterflies to sunlit petals,
enchanted by the zeal in her laughter.

in her nurturing presence,
we find safety.
her love, a sanctuary.
her spirit, a protective barrier.

in my mother's hands was me,
a tiny life born of God's mercy,
carried by a faith that love,
even when scarred,
was still love.
still worth holding,
still deserving of faith.

my mother knew forgiveness
before she understood healing.
she firmly believes
that love demands effort.
refusing to surrender
to the troubles it faces.

watching her hurt
made me believe differently.
if love truly conquers all,
there should be no wars to make peace.
love wasn't designed to hurt;
if it does, then it can't be love.

my mother taught me
to trust the hands of family.
that family isn't bound by blood,
but by the ones God places beside you.

through trials and misunderstandings,
even when their hands tremble,
even when they fumble their hold,
they remain.
they're the ones who stay.

my mother's hands are the home I know,
the roots from which my spirit grows.
in every touch I feel His plans,
etched in the strength
of my mother's hands.

I heard I love you
from both my mother and father,
but it never landed the same.

my mother's love
lived in the color of her words,
in the warmth of her touch,
in the way she held me close,
making sure I knew I was cherished.
she taught me something more,
her love was only a glimpse
of something bigger,
something beyond us.

I love you,
but Jesus loves you more, she'd say.
I knew her love, felt it.
it pointed me toward a love
that transcended what we shared.

my father's love was harder to feel.
the words, I love you
felt like a formality,
something said because it had to be.

when he spoke of love,
it carried anger, control,
and a dismissal of anything
that didn't fit into the life
he had mapped out for me.
with him, I learned to hold back.

I love you became something I'd say
when it felt required
not because I didn't mean it,
but because I didn't know
if he ever meant it back.
I couldn't trust his affection,
it felt like fragile glass,
always on the verge of shattering.
and I was afraid
of being the one to break it.

my father's shoulders
bore the strain of generations,
the stress making him bow
instead of rise.
the last of ten,
he was raised by hands
trembling under loss.
a father's absence
casting shadows over his childhood.

the echoes of a father's voice,
silenced too soon,
left his older brothers
as fragile pillars.
a mother's love
stretched too thin to mend.
he reached for love,
only to grasp empty air.

my father learned to stand tall,
from the need to survive.
his shoulders wide
yet bent with longing,
strained beneath the ache
of proving his worth.

with each passing year,
they grew heavier.
burdened by unspoken fears,
scarred by a love
he was never shown to trust.

in the eyes that watched,
pain lingered like an unanswered prayer.
my father placed his worth
in the weight of gold,
counting success in coins,
not in laughter.
the world taught him to measure
himself by what he lacked,
and he believed it.

to him,
strength was in possessions,
a dream louder than wisdom.
he spoke of riches yet to come,
boasting of ideas not yet formed,
casting his vision into jealous winds
that swept it away
before it could take root.

to admit fear was to admit defeat.
so he turned to those
who offered false sanctuaries,
their smiles sharp as knives,
their words dripping with deceit.

a man, unhealed, hid his fears
behind the glare of his stare,
burdened by a life
that never felt enough.

even in the eyes that watched,
something sacred remained—
a glimpse of a child,
still waiting to be seen.
and in his quiet yearning,
I see the faint outlines
of the man he was meant to be.

lielle amorét

he was a father,
but not the kind I prayed for.
his love was heavy, sharp-edged,
wrapped in silence and discipline.

I used to see him as anger incarnate,
a man who poured his fears into us,
his words cutting instead of building.
I didn't know then
that he spoke from his pain.

in my father's silence,
is a branch where pain takes root,
its stem spreading like ivy,
twisting over the bare soil of his soul.

he speaks not to us,
but to the world beyond our walls,
seeking solace in harmful hands.
his heart is a door left ajar,
opening to the wrong roads,
leading him further from our love.

in his silence, there is a throb.
a beating heart that extends for us,
though tangled in the thorns
of his regrets.

I believe in the One
who speaks life into barren places,
who breathes green
into withered branches.
no curse, no shadow, no limitation,
is too great for His mercy to undo.

may His love find my father,
as winter surrenders to spring.
the frost of his anger
melting into rivers of grace,
the bare branches breaking into bloom.

let the flowers rise as blessings,
each petal a promise,
each leaf a testament,
that even the longest winter
can't withstand the warmth of His light.

from the outside, they were pristine,
their silence
painted a picture of harmony.
each gesture deliberate,
each smile rehearsed.
but when the curtains closed
and the shadows found their voice,
my father's voice was a tide,
rising only in storms,
its force carving cracks
in the perfect tableau.

his words were sharp,
cutting through her quiet endurance.
he loved her
in the way silence loves a room;
filling the space yet leaving it hollow.

in my mother's hands,
she took in more than her share,
the heaviness of his fears,
his unspoken apologies,
and a love he was never taught to carry.

he was the one to pull the seams,
but also the one
to fear their unraveling.
only when the pressure of her pain
escaped her lips,
did he remember to love her;
a love tied to the fear of losing her.

she became the keeper of his storms,
standing firm while his winds howled,
fighting the clouds
that tried to consume him whole.

I grew up listening to their duets,
his voice would rise,
and hers would follow, until a bridge
wove itself between them.

I watched her guard him,
even when he didn't deserve it,
because she chose to love him
in a way he couldn't love himself.
she prayed for peace to find him,
even as his storms raged on.

God opened my eyes to his brokenness,
to the restrained,
concealed traumas he carried.
the pressure of being more
lingered in every step he took.
it was never about me.
it was about him,
fighting battles I couldn't see.
love, not judgment, was the remedy.

I see him at the crossroads,
ready to embrace the man he is,
the beautiful soul who, like me,
is trying, is struggling,
is finding meaning in his purpose.

and in this moment,
I choose to walk with him
from a place of patience,
from a place of understanding,
and most importantly,
from a place of peace.

this is my crossroads:
where the road of resentment ends,
and the path of unconditional love
begins.

I understand him as a precious soul,
a boy still searching for love
in a world that left him behind.

the roads he walked
were never paved with ease;
his anger wasn't a choice,
but the voice of a child,
crying out for love in the wrong ears,
trapped in a house
that was never built to be a home.

to honor my father doesn't mean
placing him on a pedestal
or carrying his wounds as my own.
it means letting go
of the expectations I once held,
and simply being the love
he wasn't taught to understand.

as I carry forward his legacy,
I strive to build a bridge of empathy,
a path where love and acceptance
pave the path for healing and growth.

I stand at the crossroads now,
no longer a child, but as a woman
who understands the heart.
the roads behind me
are lined with lessons,
a brick in the foundation
of who I am today,
and who I will become.

at this crossroad,
I no longer wait for validation
from hands never meant to give it.

I have learned to walk it without fear.
I now know that love
doesn't demand perfection,
it only asks for presence.

I'm an intersection
of the past and future.
my parents' love was unsteady, tampered
by the damage of their household,
and I became the glue.

my mother gave her all,
but my father's anger left its mark.
I learned to protect, shield,
and be the child and the guardian.

my siblings, doe-eyed and trusting,
look to me for answers,
but I'm still learning
what it means to love, forgive,
and hold a family together
without breaking myself.

born into a lineage of survival,
I put up with the burden
of their dreams:
my father's need for validation,
my mother's wish to mend the broken.

their hardship swayed my route,
and I pursued it without question
until God reminded me that my journey
was meant to be uniquely mine.

listen to the people
who call you pretty.
the ones who say it softly,
at random moments
especially when you feel
anything but that.

believe the words that show up
when you're not trying,
when your head is down
and your guard is up.

trust the "weird" kids,
the awkward kind ones
who saw you before you saw yourself.
the "popular" ones only pick at you
because they can't understand
how you shine without trying.
they don't get how someone like you
can glow brighter than their following.
but one day, you will.

you'll look in the mirror
and recognize the same girl
you used to call ugly.
you'll love her smile,
the one someone else loved first.
and you'll understand that the thing
that made you magnetic was always favor,
the kind God gives
without needing permission.

~   an ode to the younger me

we began as young and obscure seeds,
rooted in different soil,
each with the potential to grow.

each seed holds fruit,
yet not every tree grows the same.
success isn't measured
by the harvest of another,
our paths are not the same.

what flourishes in one
may struggle to bloom in another,
though that doesn't make its spring
any less radiant.

we are not bound to replicate
the destinies others have walked;
within our adversities
lies our unique victory.

the roots we plant today will bear fruit
in their own time and way,
and that harvest will be ours to claim.

love is both a noun and a verb.
it's the art of love
and the act of loving.
we're the embodiment of art,
a masterpiece in the making.
though in the act of loving,
we often lose ourselves.

dear reader,

maybe love came gently for you.
maybe you were watered and not wrung dry.
that's beautiful, don't dim it.
you're a reminder that love can be safe.
that security isn't boring, it's holy.

> love is patient, love is kind...
> it always protects, always trusts,
> always hopes, always perseveres.
> (1 Corinthians 13:4-7)

you may not know what it's like
to fear love's return.
and that doesn't make you soft.
sometimes I wonder how it feels
to trust the fall.

if you've known that kind of love
don't water it down.
don't hide it in an attempt to blend in.
you were loved well.
you're not naive, you're sacred.
you're what I am learning to believe in.

read.

know.

grow.

epiphora

tears fall like rain,
soaking the earth beneath
of what was left unsaid

my life felt like a mess,
a tone-deaf song played out of tune.

but in every broken note,
love abides,
gathering the shards, singing,
even this can become music.

I loved love,
the way I loved the stars
distant, untouchable,
a mystery to trace with my eyes
when the night wrapped the earth
in its velvet arms.

I loved love,
in its silent constellations,
I thought it would arrive to fill me,
like stardust drifting on cosmic tides.

I loved love,
believing it was a guiding star
in my darkness,
therapy for the broken places.
I thought it would come like dawn
to meet me at the horizon.

in our house, anger wasn't a whisper.
it was a nuclear weapon
never waiting for the right moment.
I didn't know how to handle it,
so I absorbed it.

I swallowed it whole,
and when it surfaced,
it wasn't even mine anymore.
it was his, hers,
and then it became mine to carry.
my anger was borrowed
from the pieces of them
that I let fester inside.

in my family, fear was foreign
a sign of deception
and spiritual failure.
I was too young to understand fear
and know it's part of life,
a signal to the soul
that help is needed.

instead of feeling seen,
I was told to suppress it, to deny it.
so I withdrew further into myself,
shying away from asking for help,
fearing that my vulnerability
would be met with judgment.

I loved my siblings fiercely.
even so,
my love carried sharp edges.
fear and irritation spilled all over,
projected onto the ones
I was meant to protect.

I dictated perfection because I feared
they'd inherit my wounds.

I was captivated by the notion
that beauty held the key to love,
to happiness.
I believed that beautiful people
had a charm, a magnet
that drew admiration and affection.

I found comfort in pretty things,
reflecting the way
people poured value into them.

more than anything,
I longed to embody
that captivating beauty,
to radiate magnetism
from every fiber of my being.

I convinced myself that physical beauty
would be the antidote to my sadness—
a fast pass to favor and validation.

I dreamed of a life
where simply existing
as my most beautiful self
would unlock doors:
opportunities, admiration,
and all forms of love.

growing up,
the mirror was my enemy.
it reflected every insult,
every insecurity.
I believed the voices
that called me ugly,
and then I became one of them.

but God showed me
a different point of view,
one of beauty, worth,
and divine creation.

reality felt too heavy,
so I retreated into illusions.
a world where the pain from home
couldn't touch me,
where I was filled with beauty,
wealth, intimacies.

then those illusions became chains,
binding me to a life
I could only imagine.
it took years to see,
that the beauty I sought
was already within me.

I dream of being loved
in a way that's rewarding and true.
being pretty isn't enough.
even with constant compliments,
why do I still feel superficial?
no amount of adoration
can make me happy,
when looking in the mirror
doesn't feel enough.

I'll be beautiful if I feel it myself.
no one's love can ever be enough
until it's mine.

me. myself. mine. and I...
why are you counting God out?

did you forget He lives in you?
when you remember the countless times
He has proven that He loves you,
shouldn't you trust to love yourself?

I learned to equate love with silence,
to see distance as safety,
and to believe that vulnerability
only opens the door to betrayal.

watching my parents, I thought love
meant enduring the pain,
not sharing it.
my father's fear of weakness
became my fear of trusting,
of opening up to anyone.

I grew up believing closeness
was a trap, that attachment was a risk
I couldn't afford.
I held people at arm's length,
craving connection,
but not believing in its loyalty.

my parents' love gave me the idea
that affection could suffocate,
that devotion carried expectations
I might fail to meet.

so I told myself
labels were the problem.
it's too confining,
too suffocating.
when really, I feared losing someone
who claimed they'd never leave.

but avoidance is lonely.
it doesn't shield, it isolates.
it keeps love out and healing away.

everything I did was for his approval,
yet no achievement, no award,
ever seemed to be enough.

he measured me in currency,
in potential wealth,
and I began to wonder
was I his daughter?
or his investment?

the people I called friends
reflected who I wanted to be:
articulate, assertive, diligent.

even though I never let them see
the darker parts of me,
I hid my pain,
pretended to be at peace,
and wondered why connection
always felt out of reach.

my mother warned me
not to trust too easily.
her words became walls,
and I locked myself inside.

friendships felt dangerous,
love felt impossible.
but slowly,
I am learning to open the door.

we began as distant constellations,
strangers,
trailing separate passages.
each star, silent,
holding secrets of its own.

then by some silent pull,
our orbits aligned,
and we became more—friends, lovers,
something in between.

bound in the warmth of shared laughter,
stories, and dreams,
close enough
to catch each other's falling light.
until somehow, we dimmed.

the pull loosened and unraveled
until we quietly drifted
two souls no longer tethered,
moving where God wills us to be.

the grief isn't in the separation,
but in clinging to what
He never meant for me to keep.
some heartbreaks are lessons
crafted by His hand,
to guide us to the love
only He can give.

I hoped for closures in them,
while the intimacy I craved
was always with Him.
their love wasn't the missing piece,
and their absence
became the space where He worked.

in letting go,
my sincere and whole love
becomes a mirror of their emptiness,
a reflection of what they lost.

love, when it's true,
is never wasted.
it transforms us, and them,
so that one day,
we'll be ready
for a love that's everlasting.

we say, "right person, wrong time,"
clinging to a hope
that the clock had betrayed us.

however, it was never about time,
it was about alignment.
God's hands don't fumble with the hours.

every meeting and every parting
is intentional, purposeful,
and tied to a plan
far beyond what we can see.

we weren't meant to last.
we were rushing for love to save us,
when love was still teaching us
to see our faults.

the lesson is in the division.
through you,
I learned what love could be:
patient, forgiving, honest.
and through me,
you learned what love demands:
commitment, trust, growth.

some days turn into feelings;
the kind you can't name, only carry.

I'll still love you the same.
like that little ache in my chest
when a memory breathes—not painful,
just enough to remind me
we'll never go back.

but it still meant something
and maybe that's all it was meant to do.

I'm sorry.
I'm sorry I couldn't show up for you
the way you showed up for me.
you celebrated my milestones,
you stood beside me in joy,
yet now, I can't return the favor.

it's not that I don't want to, I do.
but my heart feels heavy,
and my spirit feels drained.
I don't want to pour
from a place of emptiness,
to give you the scraps
of what should be intact.

I wish I could love you with all of me,
but I have fragments right now.
and you deserve more than that.

and maybe it's my fault.
I've never been good
at communicating my emotions.
I struggle to find
the words that won't hurt,
words that won't confuse,
words that could help you understand
why I've retreated.

it's hard to explain I need to be away,
don't take it
as my lack of love for you,
I'm just not in a place of wellness.

pretending to be okay
wouldn't serve either of us.
sharing the complexity of my struggles
might cast a shade on your light.

it grieves me—
this distance I've created.
I romanticize my friendships,
dream of adoring you
the way you deserve.
but right now, I need time.

if I can't be sincere or show up fully,
I'd rather retreat
to a place where I can recharge.
I'm trying to be better,
a better person, a better friend.

I hope you understand.
if you don't,
I hope you find peace in leaving.
because love isn't waiting in the cold
while I watch you from inside,
in the asylum of my solitude.

to those who stay, thank you.
to those who leave, I still love you.

I pray for you, my friends
that we'll meet in abundance.
our cups will overflow,
and we'll pour out of love,
peace, and grace.
for each other,
as well as for the world around us.

at the moment, my only refuge is God.
He can fill the space I've left vacant,
and at the same time,
fill the space I've left for Him alone.
I confide in Him,
because He can be everywhere,
anywhere, all at once.

I'm a lone wolf, it seems.
I love passionately, genuinely,
but when I lose myself,
I run to the only place
where I can be refilled,
in the arms of my God.

my insecurities screamed
that I was unworthy
and would only be satisfied
if the world loved me first.

but there was a version of me,
that only God could see,
eternally aligned with His riches.
He spoke it into being,
and all I asked for in His name
was already mine.

to my soul, listen closely:
death isn't your peace.
it won't erase your pain.
it'll simply cast it into the void,
like a blob of ink
spilled across an unfinished story.

doesn't it enrage the author?
doesn't it leave a nasty mark,
a smell of a mistake unresolved?
it seeps through the pages,
ruining a story that would've been
published, fulfilled, and admired.

your suffering wouldn't vanish,
it would only become a ghost,
haunting the chapters left unwritten.

I won't let our story end like that.
the world desperately needs
the depth, love, and light in us.

if we were to end now,
we won't be remembered
for the beauty we carried,
but for the act of ending it all.
the headlines would label us:
another life lost to despair.

and while the subtext
might nod to our agony,
the complexity of our pain—
our joy interlaced with melancholy,
would remain unread.

because the joy was there,
in the laughter that resonated
between tears,
the goofy jokes, the playful pranks,
the lighthearted moments
that felt like any other day
yet meant the world.

it was there,
in the way we leaned
into each other's cultures,
exchanging dreams,
interests, and values,
watching the smile in their eyes
from being noticed and respected.

it was there,
in the way we loved despite the flaws,
when someone revealed a truth
they had kept hidden.
we listened,
letting the moment caress us.

the joy was there
in the unexpected attachment,
when our love overpowered pain
and even the silence between us
felt safe.

to end it now
would erase the profound beauty
we've witnessed, the persistence
and the shared spaces
that made life real.
our story deserves more
than an abrupt ending;
it deserves the redemption of a finale,
where every ecstasy and depression
is sewn into something eternal.

let me tell you this, my soul:
suicide isn't rebellion,
it's not freedom.
it murders the innocence,
destroys the love we've poured out,
and shatters the hearts
that prayed for us.

it erases the promise of a life
we once dreamed of creating.
it mutes the laughter
that was yet to come,
and buries the hope God planted in us.

God's promise is still valid:
your present suffering doesn't compare
to the glory that lies ahead.

this pain,
as heavy as it feels,
is meant to teach us to love
even when it hurts,
and find power in that love.

don't let the voice of death
deceive you.
don't let it convince you
that it's the only way out.
it's an illusion, an escape from a life
that isn't meant to end this way.

so what is it that we want, my soul?
how do we want to love
and be loved in return?
indulge in that passion.
find what makes the heart
burn with purpose.

is it the arts?
is it in giving?
is it the vibes of the night,
the giggles that erupts
when life feels too serious?

if it's me you're displeased with,
then forgive me.
forgive me for failing to honor you,
for doubting our strength.
hold on to us
we're all we have and worth saving.

God is in us, and we abide in Him,
His Spirit heals the moments
we thought would break us.
there's no way we can fail.

one day, those who doubted us,
hurt us, or dismissed us will wonder,
how did we glow so brightly?
how did we find peace
when the world tried to tame us?

I want to be there with you, my soul,
when we bask in the love
that feels like home.
coddle in pleasures that heal:
the enticing existence of the moon,
the jazz of rainy days,
the freedom of knowing
we don't need to conform.

sacrifice the pain of yesterday.
surrender tomorrow to God.
and let us remain here,
in the pulchritude and chaos of today.
to live is to be loved,
and to love is to persist;
for ourselves,
and He who anticipates our return.

it's a blessing
to be loved by you, my soul.
and it's a blessing to be loved by me.

when will the crying end?
when will I finally articulate
what I'm truly feeling,
being honest with myself?
when will I be comfortable
with making mistakes?
why can't I take the advice I give out?

I need a way out,
but I keep closing the door.
I'm tired of myself,
yet I want better for myself.
I need someone
but I don't want anyone near.

it's frustrating
when things don't go my way.
but is that important?
is that worth ruining my day over it?
is that worth the irritation?
I can feel however I feel,
so why is it so wrong?
why does guilt linger in these moments?
what is the right way to deal with this?

I asked Him for serenity,
why isn't He responding?
or is there too much noise
in my mind to hear Him?
I want this chapter of my life to end,
before I harm the things
I wish to repair.

it's always don't lose faith,
but faith isn't lost, I am.
faith hasn't abandoned me,
I've strayed too far to grasp it.
the faith is there,
I just can't catch up.

my mind, soul, and body are at war,
fighting separate battles
on the same battlefield.
I need them to unite,
but they're all speaking
in different tongues,
pulling me in different directions.

I say to myself,
it's okay to feel tired, conflicted,
and uncertain about how to proceed.
that tension between
wanting better for myself
and feeling stuck is a sign of growth,
even if it doesn't feel like it now.

it's not wrong to feel what I'm feeling.
guilt and frustration are from the idea
that I should handle things
a certain way.
emotions are messengers, not masters.
they're not something to fight against,
but to sit with,
to hear what they're saying
beneath the surface.

when I say, faith has lost sight of me,
it's a poignant reflection
of how disconnected I feel
being held by it.

God's serenity is not absent.
sometimes it's quieter
than the storm in my mind.
in moments like this, it's not about
trying harder to hear Him,
but allowing myself to be still,
even in the confusion.

I'm not broken for feeling this way.
my mind, soul, and body feel at odds,
yet they all want the same thing:
peace, healing, unity.
their dissonance doesn't mean
they can't work together;
it's a signal that something deeper
needs tending.

I may be in a battlefield,
but battles are fought
because victory is possible.

I'm not giving up
on the part of me that wants better,
the part that reminds me I'm my keeper,
carrying a Spirit greater than myself.
I can't fail her.
she knows our destiny,
and holds me
to the greatness she sees in me.

it's time I admit I am where I am,
because of my wrong decisions.
I am where I am,
because I let things happen to me
instead of standing firm
and making things happen for me.

I admit, I was too lazy
to build toward my future,
convincing myself
the future me would figure it out,
neglecting that my future me
was waiting on the actions
of present me.

I chose mediocrity in Christianity
to please the world,
making excuses for my actions
and indulging in what it offered,
even as guilt whispered
I was losing myself.

I admit that I chose not to pray,
blaming time,
instead of the disorder
of my priorities.
I blamed my pain and depression
on demons,
but the truth is,
they never had power over me.
I was comfortable with being weak.
I co-signed and cooperated with them
to bring me to this state.

when I felt like the world hated me,
I remember it hated Him first too.
Jesus faced the weight of rejection,
the sting of betrayal, the loneliness
of being misunderstood.

despite it all, He loved anyway.
He forgave anyway.
He kept going on anyway.
when the world turns its back,
I don't let it harden my heart.
their hate isn't the measure
of my soul, His love is.

dear reader,

I shut down when things get too close.
you lean in harder.
you offer more than you're asked for,
hoping it'll be enough to make someone stay.
but love isn't earned through exhaustion.
you don't have to prove your worth
to be chosen.
God already chose you.

"before I formed you in the womb, I knew you."
(Jeremiah 1:5)

I know you're afraid that love will leave,
but His perfect love casts out fear.
I hold back to protect myself,
you overextend to preserve the love.
but neither of us needs to fight to be seen
when He saw us first.

passion lights the fire,
commitment keeps it burning,
pleasure reminds us of the feeling in the light,
and sacrifice, the willing surrender
that waxes it all together

I thought love was loud.
a declaration,
an aura too captivating to look away.
I searched for it
in the voices of others,
in the echoes of my longing,
only to be met with silence.

I mistook the quiet for emptiness,
for absence, for being forsaken.
but Love saw me through,
lingering patiently
until I understood Him.
teaching me that silence
was never the absence of Love
it was the noise of Him staying.

love, in its purest form,
isn't defined by the failures of others,
but by the light we choose
to move forward.

love is the difference
between simply existing
and truly living.
love isn't a passive feeling,
but an active practice, demonstrated
through actions and honesty.

we're called to love like Him.
to love without conditions, selflessly.
this is the foundation of all love,
which starts with Him
and flows through us.

when love knocked, I didn't open,
because love looked fleeting.
if love were real,
it would break down the door,
prove its strength in grand displays.
but love doesn't force itself in.
it knocks.
and I,
convinced that love must be chased,
stood on the other side,
with a straight-face attitude,
waiting for it to prove its worth.

yet Love already had proof
on a hill, on a bloodstained cross
and an empty grave.

love looks like safety,
like being held in someone's arms,
even if only for a fleeting moment.
in that instant, you're seen,
you're valued.

love with another
doesn't always last forever.
some relationships fade,
some grow apart.
but in those moments of connection,
real love is felt.

love looks like making others
feel appreciated, comfortable,
at home in your presence.
it looks like smiling
with your whole self,
liberating yourself from insecurities,
and letting joy in.

love looks like a smile,
the kind that escapes
when you forget to care.
I saw it in a picture once.
there I was, gap-toothed,
smiling with everything I had.

I loved how I looked in that moment—
free from social anxiety,
free from the constraints
of a personality I had shaped
to protect my image,
to avoid being perceived
in ways I feared.
at peace,
surrounded by those I cared for,
alive with enthusiasm.

my love for the arts burned brightly,
but my father's voice extinguished it.
it won't bring in money, he said.

so, I silenced my passions,
trading my dreams for a path
I was conditioned to choose.
despite that, the fire never truly died.
in my high school halls I saw glimpses
of the star I could've been,
the stages I never performed on,
the characters I never embodied.
all of it lost to fear— fear of failure,
fear of being seen.
what would've happened
if I had just let myself shine?

finding peace within myself
began with releasing the grip of regret,
and loosening the fear
of what's to come.
it's a surrender to the present,
where life truly unfolds.

when I anchor myself in the now,
I break free
from the shadows of yesterday,
and the weight of tomorrow,
allowing myself to live
authentically, unbothered.

finding peace with God
is trusting in the unseen,
knowing that every trial and moment
is pieced into greater glory.

despite the chaos I see now,
success, favor, and prosperity
are my birthright.
in surrendering my doubts,
I walk confidently,
knowing He goes before me,
aligning every step with His purpose.
and in that trust,
peace becomes my inheritance.

I never meant to become distant
I just learned to feel safe
in my isolation.
needing no one felt like survival,
so I convinced myself it was strength.
I mastered detachment
until love felt unfamiliar
and care felt suspicious.

sometimes I'd rather disappear
than risk being misunderstood.
yet even when I withdrew, He stayed.
even when I questioned His presence,
He never turned away.
He gave me certainty,
that no matter what choice I make,
He will never leave nor forsake me.

I see myself in you;
in the sound of your laugh,
your anger and the outbursts
that remind me of who I used to be.

I shouldn't be upset when you act
in ways that frustrate me.
I once held
that same temper and stubbornness,
and maybe, in some ways, I still do.
if anything, I should feel honored.
you mirror the parts of me
I still need to understand.

when you like the things I like,
when you wear my style,
when you speak with phrases
I thought were mine alone,
it's not to take my light.
it's your way of saying,
I admire you,
and this is how I make it my own.

in your eyes, you're a shadow of me.
I'll step aside, push you to the front,
and cheer you on from the back.
I've sometimes pushed you away
when you wanted to be close to me.

God, in His humor, designed you
not just as my siblings,
but as friends I wouldn't have chosen,
all the same,
friends I would never trade.

you've taught me to speak
as if I'm speaking to myself.
though we all look alike,
your beauty is yours alone.
your fire, light, and love
are all uniquely yours.
I'm just here to make sure
you shine even brighter.

      - in endless love, your big sister

loving you has been like
gazing into a kaleidoscope.
at first glance,
it's difficult to see clearly.
a swirl of colors and shapes,
shifting too fast
to make sense of it all.

but when I look closer and focus
on the light breaking through,
I see the patterns hidden within.
I see the childlike innocence in you,
peeking through the gap.
I see it in how you dance,
in the stories of your youth,
and in those rare moments
when joy overtakes you,
and your body laughs.
those are the colors I cherish.

I don't love, though,
when shadows cloud the view.
when spirits dim your light,
and the patterns blur into calamity.

I don't love when your words pierce deep
or when you tell me
I don't love or respect you.
I wish you could see the colors in me
and the ways I've tried to honor you
even when I don't understand you.

I don't love
when you feel distant from us,
when it feels as if money
is your peace of mind,
while this tailing chase
is taking away pieces of mine.

the relentless pursuit of wealth
seems to place it above all else.
we are treated as just another expense,
our needs weighed in the balance,
our emotional well-being
overlooked for financial gain.

it feels as if
our connection and presence
are no longer priorities
but rather secondary considerations,
sacrificed to secure more.

in the beginning, love found me

we're specks of your kaleidoscope,
and how you turn toward us
determines how we shine.
why is it feeling
like you value your friends
more than us most of the time,
as if the connection we share
isn't enough to pull you in?
do you see how wealthy you are already?
or is our presence
not perceived for what it is?

I have so much grace to give you,
I know there's more to you
than the pain that speaks for you.
I pray to set you free from the turmoil
that clouds your peace.

I want to show you a love that soothes
the harsh glare of shifting colors.
a love that doesn't falter,
a love that doesn't speak evil of you
when you turn away.

I want to show you
a love worth staying sober for,
a love so vivid and undivided
that surpasses anything
you've ever dreamed of.

I want you to see yourself
through God's eyes,
because you're loved,
even when you doubt it.
I see your kaleidoscope,
every divine, broken,
and intelligent piece of it,
and I love you even more.

I want to love you well,
even through the turbulence,
because above all else,
you're the only dad
I will have in this life.

    - with all my heart, your firstborn

I love how you love
unapologetically, pathetically,
without pride or restriction.
you don't care if loving us
makes you look foolish.
you choose love, every time,
and it's the most beautiful thing.

I'm blessed to call you mom every day.
it's not just a word,
it's a testament to the love
you've poured into me.
to say mom is to remember the times
you showed me what love looks like.

my favorite memory of us
was when my heart was broken
beyond words, and I was grieving
silently in my dark room.
you didn't ask questions.
you came to me,
lifted my head onto your lap,
and embraced me as I cried.
the only sound escaping from the room
were the strings of my heart.

another memory that stays with me
is when all hope felt lost,
my mind was confused,
and I was declaring revelations
that weren't from God.
then God sent the real sign to me,
your voice.
you said you love me,
despite who the pain
was telling me I was.
you said I am free to be as I am,
and your love holds no expectations.

you are mine, you cried.
you said I am one of the strengths
that keeps you going,
because sometimes you, too,
want an easy way out.
but where would that leave us?

you told me you would do anything
in your power for me.
and in that moment,
I saw the depth of your love,
a love that holds no context.

I don't love when you take on
more than you bear.
when the haunting of pains
stalks the halls of your joy.
I see the strain it puts on you,
and it hurts,
because all I can do is pray.

I pray you feel peace every day,
not just in the days of good news.
I pray you find peace in aging,
a body that doesn't always move
as you intend.
I pray for healing, so your body moves
just as it was designed to.
you don't need any more suffering,
not in your body or your heart.
it scares me, if I'm being honest,
when your body
sends up flares of concern.

but I have faith
in the God of restoration,
the God of healing,
the God you introduced me to.
I pray to Him, and trust in His power
for your breakthrough.

I pray for those
who have wished you harm,
that they find peace within themselves.
I pray you see love,
love in the vastness that exists beyond
the adoration of your children,
love beyond your circumstances,
beyond your agony.

I know that with your endurance,
you can be an aspiration
to those who wear the same crown.
your story is beautiful,
and I can't wait for your world
to celebrate and honor you
in the way you deserve.

    — with all my love, your best friend

we may be our parents' seeds,
but we are not our parents.
the apple may not fall
far from the tree,
but eventually detaches from the branch.

I pushed some people away
due to the shadows
cast by their parents.
the actions and beliefs
of those who raised them
were assumed to define them.
the truth is,
the children carry no blame
for the choices
of those who raised them.

it's easy
to fall into the trap of judgment,
especially when disappointment
from one generation
spills over to the next.

commitment to love
means stepping away from the temptation
to hold someone's past against them.
it became a tendency
to view them through the lens
of their parents' toxic behaviors,
not realizing that they too
were enduring parallel struggles,
a feeling I know too well.

the pain they carried from a broken home
wasn't their fault.
they were not the embodiment
of their parents' choices,
yet they were judged as they were.
our parents' failures
don't write our future.
it takes commitment
to let go of the past,
to separate the child
from their family's history.
it's necessary to choose to see them
for who they are now,
not for the mess of their upbringing.

the greatest and worst advice
I have ever heard was:
it's okay to be selfish,
when you've been selfless all your life.

at first, it felt like liberation,
like chains slipping from my wrists,
permission to finally breathe
for myself.
but as I clutched the words,
they pricked the surface of my skin,
piercing through layers with a slow,
stinging pressure.
each repetition sank inwards,
spreading through me,
leaving behind an ache I couldn't numb.

when is it okay to be selfish?
how do you take back
the pieces you gave away
without feeling guilty?

I spent years pouring out,
never asking for anything in return,
until the well ran dry,
leaving me with a hollow feeling.
was I wrong for giving so much?
for loving too hard, too deeply?

the advice feels like consent
to take back what's mine.
but is it selfish
to need space to breathe,
to demand peace for my soul,
to reclaim the love I've lost in others?

the internal war of selfless love
versus the bitter cost
of keeping nothing for myself,
how do I know when it's enough?
when have I given enough of me
to the world,
and when is it time to say,
this is mine, this is for me?

I want to learn the balance,
the fierce strength
of protecting what's left,
without losing the essence of who I am.
at this point the line is blurry,
and I walk it,
torn between the pain
of giving too much,
and the shame of taking it all back.

before we can change the world,
we have to learn how to sit with it,
like Jesus did.
this doesn't mean condoning everything.
it means leading with love
so healing can begin.

Jesus never excused sin,
but He also never led with condemnation.
He met people in love,
and saw what we fail to see,
that love changes people
more than judgment ever will.

His love was radical, transformative.
it reached those who felt unworthy,
reminding them that God's love
knows no bounds.

I've learned that love and truth
aren't at war.
truth without love becomes harsh.
love without truth becomes hollow.
but love that flows
from the heart of Christ carries both.

I commit to my role as a lover of Christ
by refusing to judge
the beliefs of others.
it doesn't affect me
if they identify as an atheist,
how they pray or worship,
or the number of sins committed
while still claiming Christianity.
none of that decreases their worth.
as long as they commit to love,
that power unifies us.

I'm not ignoring sin.
I'm choosing not to weaponize it.
judgment is God's job.
mine is to love the way He does.

I love all
regardless of people's sexualities,
religions, genders, and beliefs.
judgment isn't mine to give.
we're called to love, to extend grace
to those who see differently,
to be the hands and feet of Christ,
in a world due for therapy.

we live by different laws,
we are preached different truths,
but the greatest commandment
I've been given is to love others
as I love myself.
so, I choose love.

there'll be things we can't agree on,
but love withstands
in the tussle of disagreements.
love doesn't seek
to conquer through arguments,
or demand conformity to my beliefs.

love remains steadfast,
even in the face of our differences.
those who are unlike me
don't need to hear
that they're unworthy of love,
especially when God's love
embraces us all equally.

to fear the Lord
is to obey His commands,
and His greatest command is clear:
to love.
so, I commit to loving deeply,
freely, and beyond boundaries.
the only language
we can all speak fluently is love.
it's universal,
it's human nature,
and it's my calling.

to love is to give,
to give is to lose time, pride, control.
it's in that loss
that we find something greater.

sacrificial love doesn't hoard.
it opens its hands,
even when the cost is high.
it doesn't seek to win,
but to restore, heal, and bring life
where there was once only pain.

I sense God
in the brushstroke of a petal,
in the sky loved by the vibrancy
of sunrise and sunset,
in the moments where beauty
stills my breath.

a vibration hums within me,
a resonance that feels holy,
is it the Spirit?
or the echo of my pleasure
recognizing its Creator?
except my flesh is at war
with this pleasure.
it incites that money will fulfill me,
indulgence will satisfy,
pride will crown me.
as if life is for feeding desires
instead of the strength of being alive.

the eyes crave,
hungry for ephemeral pleasures.
the flesh urges,
aching to be supplied.
the pride of life affirms,
be more, have more.

nevertheless, the soul speaks serenely
persistently:
I am abundant.
I never lack.

this clash between my spirit
and the beings of my flesh
pulls me toward the truth.
the fruit of God's love
isn't in the lust of the eyes,
the impermanent desires of the body,
nor in pride's shallow victories.

joy is rooted in gratitude.
gratitude for imperfection,
for God's attribution of my talents
and for the originality of my design,
which originated from the One
who makes no mistakes.

I enjoy acknowledging Him in others,
in nature, in every introspection
where eternity feels close.
the Spirit lives in this recognition.
and when I take the time
to speak life into those around me,
I feel the vibration of heaven,
not momentary, but eternal,
a joy that no external craving
could satisfy.

patience doesn't omit frustration,
it's the decision to breathe through it.
to love with patience
is to sit in the tension of unmet needs,
to wait for the flower to bloom
without tugging at the stem.

it's saying,
your imperfections don't scare me away,
and I won't rush your growth.

patience
is the perpetual heartbeat of love,
a pulse that never halts.

self-pity is a thief of love.
it turns your gaze inward,
blinding you to the beauty around you,
the blessings already given.

when I let self-pity in,
it convinced me that love
had no place in my struggles.
I lamented in this lie,
waiting for life to fix itself.
but love doesn't wait.
it's active, alive,
and a force that refuses
to be diminished by obscure seasons.

self-pity is a rejection of the truth
that I am created by a God
who works all things for my good.
so now, when self-pity knocks,
I meet it with love.

I remember the One
who gave everything for me,
whose love was sacrificial,
unyielding, eternal.

my struggles are not my identity.
I am loved,
and I am called to love in return.
self-pity has no place
where love resides.
because where there is love,
there is hope,
and where there is hope,
there is life.

I used to believe
that if I wasn't in control,
I was failing.
I carried the weight of expectations,
worries, anxieties,
and the invisible pressure
to meet a standard I didn't set.

overthinking consumed me,
and crying became my refuge
until it wasn't.
I cried so much, it hurt to cry.

there's a moment
when the pain stops feeling cathartic
and starts feeling suffocating.
that's when it hit me,
this isn't how I'm meant to live.
it hurts
because it's not mine to sustain.

these torments, these emotions,
were never meant to define me.
I had to stop romanticizing pain
as proof of my strength.
I surrendered, not out of weakness,
but of wisdom.

if God doesn't do it, it won't get done.
and I meant it.
this wasn't some satirical escape,
a way to avoid responsibility.
it was an act of faith.

I gave the things above me
to the One above all things.
that doesn't mean
they have power over me,
it means they belong
in the hands of someone greater.

I used to side-eye authority,
wondering if submitting
meant giving up my strength,
my ability to shape my destiny.
but submission to God isn't weakness.
it's consciousness.

I accept His power
as a strength far greater
than anything I could ever muster.
He is a God of riches,
not fleeting possessions,
but peace, wisdom, and abundance
that the world can never offer.

I let go, not because I am small,
but because He is greater.
and in His greatness, I find rest.
His patience is a soft strength,
a willingness to endure
insult and rejection,
to bear the sting of our coldness,
in the hope that we will warm up to Him.

He doesn't demand immediate change.
He invites, slowly revealing Himself,
layer by layer, until we see His face.
it's in His longsuffering
that I find the grace to repent,
the chance to open my eyes
to a love that never abandons,
but waits for my return.

I don't understand
the complexities of love.
I'm still learning how to love,
but what I'm certain about is
God is love.

dear reader,

I run when it's too real.
you run because it's real.
sometimes love feels
like both a craving and a threat.
you want to be known,
but fear the moment someone truly sees you.

me, I silence the ache.
you scream it quietly, behind a smile
that keeps shifting.
you may have been touched by pain
disguised as affection.
but God doesn't love like man does.

the Lord is close to the brokenhearted
and saves those who are crushed in spirit.
(Psalms 34:18)

you can let the walls down.
not all closeness will break you.
not all hands are here to hurt.

He heals the wounds
of every shattered heart.
(Psalms 147:3)

if love has felt confusing,
let His be the standard.
not chaotic, uncertain or unstable,
but the same yesterday, today, and forever.
(Hebrews 13:8)

odyssey

fear fades into the horizon
as love pulls me like a tide
still learning to swim

fools don't fall in love;
they fall for what they think love is
and what sense does a fool have?

the world raises us to chase reflections
and settle for illusions
of what love should be.
led by their desires,
fools fall into the trap
of chasing what isn't real.

fools confuse possession
with connection,
lust with intimacy,
approval with affection.
they mistake longing for love,
when it only mirrors fear of being
alone.

loving doesn't distort,
it doesn't imitate.
it's raw and honest,
requiring us to see clearly,
both ourselves and the ones we love.

it's not a trap but a solution,
an invitation to step away
from illusions
and into the illumination
of what's real.

I was robbed.
a thief crept into my mind
and left me blind.
it stole the moments
meant for stillness,
the peace of being mindful
of the present,
the simplicity of each breath,
each sight, and every sound
that could anchor me to now.

I was a child,
dreaming of tomorrows that never came.
the thief promised a life
painted in perfection,
a version of myself so far ahead,
I made no steps toward her.

I couldn't see the beauty of who I was,
too busy chasing the mirage
of who I thought I should be.

the thief robbed me of childhood,
of being present in the small joys,
of giving gratitude
for the struggles that were shaping me.
instead, I drifted,
always elsewhere, never here.

I look back and see
the thief's fingerprints on my years.
I understand it now,
the cost of its lies.
I have God to thank
for revealing this truth:
love is the greatest journey.

it's not too late,
there's time to reclaim what was stolen.
the past taught me who I could've been,
but today reminds me
who I can still become.

growing up,
I thought my parents didn't understand.
they had no idea
what I was going through.
now that I'm more than a child,
and less than a parent,
I can see both sides
of this misunderstanding.

parents see the world
through layers of trials,
errors, trauma, and resilience.
they see problems in widescreen—
ten dimensions of wellness,
ten decades of worry.

but a child's world is small.
so even small problems
feel like the end of the world.
what they called "nothing,"
was everything to me.
somewhere along the way
we tipped the scale,
saw the world as it really is,
and forgot how big it used to feel.

I wish they could've remembered
what it was like to be me.
I wish they knew how dismissive it felt.
how hypocritical,
to be told to "grow up"
by people who were once just as soft.

maybe they couldn't even afford
to be soft when they were kids.
maybe they had to raise themselves.
I get that now.
both sides need grace.

I can see how their childhoods
shaped how they love.
I can see how their rules
were all they knew about survival.

I'm glad to have my parents as mine.
I'm even more glad
their parents didn't raise me.
no shade.

I just wish
they would give their children
the honor they longed themselves.
it means something to be seen,
heard, and understood.

I see it with my siblings.
and sometimes,
I catch myself copying the same critique
that used to wound me.
I forget how it felt until I remember,
it wasn't so long ago I was them.

I remember thinking
the only way to get their attention
was through extreme action.
it was only
when my life seemed in danger
that their parenting kicked in.
but even then,
nothing really changed.

sometimes,
a child doesn't hide their pain
to shield their parents,
they just want to be taken seriously.
"how would I know
if you don't say anything?"
doesn't work when I've said it
and you still don't hear me.

I didn't want to protect you
from my truth,
I just wanted you to believe it.
I look back and wish I cried less.
I wish I said things with less sass,
and more trust in the process.
I wish someone reminded me I had time.
time to grow,
time to bloom,
time to just be a kid.

we'll never be kids again
in this lifetime,
so let them be kids.
let them feel and express freely
without shame
or correction at every turn.

protect the youth
in ways they won't understand
until they're grown,
looking back
at the little versions of themselves.

and the cycle continues
with growing up...
thinking the parent wouldn't understand.
while the parent believes
they already do,
forgetting that what feels small to them
is everything to someone still learning
the meaning of their world.

she's getting older now.
sometimes she's full of energy,
and other times
she can barely get out of bed.
I feel helpless,
wishing there was more I could do.

there are moments she misremembers,
but I don't correct her.
I don't want her to notice
the small gaps in her memory.
a pang settles in my chest
as I watch her lean on supplements
to support her aging body.

I wish I could stop time,
keep her youthful,
protect her from the passing years.
but aging is as natural as the seasons,
and even now she's as beautiful as ever.
her age doesn't reflect her appearance,
still pressure,
still glowing,
still her.

her prime is everlasting,
and I'm determined to make
the second half of her life,
her golden era.

she's faced so much, took in too much,
and now, it's her time to live.
she sowed seeds of faith
her entire life,
planting her trust in the Lord.
there are many things I ask of Him,
but if I could choose just one,
I pray He grants her
the harvest she's been promised.

she taught me my first everything.
it's my turn to honor her,
to rise in a standing ovation.
crown her with awards of praise,
and fly to the sky
to pluck any star she wants.

there's much left for us to share,
and everyday with her is sacred.
lately,
time is moving ridiculously fast.
but I trust the God we both look to,
the One whose name we call.
He promises long life and salvation,
and in Him, I place my hope for her.

I owe you an apology, Daddy.
I've said I understand you now,
but there were so many things
I couldn't see before.
I see the anchor that pulled you down,
but I failed to acknowledge
the ways I added to that sinking burden.

you don't owe me an apology
for the things we went through.
yes, you've hurt me,
you've hurt all of us.
but if I were to sit and list
every way you've wounded me,
it wouldn't be the book of love anymore.

I've made peace within my heart,
but I still need to come to you,
to ask for your forgiveness.
I see the love you give,
the sacrifices you made,
and I want you to know
I appreciate it all.
I'm proud of you, Daddy.

I see you changing day by day,
growing into the father
you're still becoming.
you've endured more than I can think of,
wanted to give up so many times,
but you stayed.
for us.
for our happiness.

in your own way,
you've been trying
to bring peace to our family.
you might have felt lost,
unsupported, unheard, unseen.
and for that, I'm sorry.

I'm sorry for not noticing you.
for neglecting the love you needed,
for all the times I disregarded the fact
that you feel pain too.

as a father, as a man,
the world expects you to be invincible.
and there were times
you seemed that way.

you sought happiness outside our home.
it's not like you didn't love us,
maybe you needed a distraction,
an escape from the burdens
that greeted you here:
the stacking bills and petty arguments,
the endless lists of provisions,
the stress
of keeping a family satisfied.
I'm sorry for dismissing that,
for belittling the weights
you had to lift.

thank you for everything.
for staying when it was hardest.
for giving when you had nothing left.
you as our father is enough.
I pray for your peace, Daddy.
to mend every scar in your heart
with the love God rests in me.

happiness begins in the mind,
and the power of our thoughts
can either lift us or break us.
manipulative thoughts corrupt me
to believe my mistakes
were all I would amount to,
that my insecurities were my truth.
but those thoughts were not mine.
they are shadows of fear,
reflections of an agony
that has lingered far too long.

I found comfort in God,
in the confidence
He wouldn't turn His back on me
for feeling how I felt.
when I spoke to Him
I didn't have to hide.
I didn't have to wear a mask.
I could just be, raw and unfiltered,
and He would listen.

in His listening,
I learned to listen to myself,
my emotions, and the love
that always surrounds me,
even in my darkest moments.

when thoughts that aren't mine creep in,
I don't react.
I imagine them as passing air,
letting them speak their piece
before they float away.
not every thought is true.
the doubts, fears,
and insecurities I clung to
are not who I am.
they are mirroring wounds,
not my essence.

the power to control them
isn't fighting back.
I conquer them
by diminishing their hold,
by refusing to let their force
settle in.
the true control is in the release,
in the peace I find in letting go.

I will not deprive my energy
on thoughts that bring me
to a state of depression.
I have free will for a reason,
I'm exercising that
by focusing on thoughts
that wish me well.

I was taught that sadness, despair, fear
were all signs of weakness.
expressing these emotions
wasn't seen as natural,
but as an invitation
for the devil to claim my heart.

so I concealed them,
locked them away deep inside,
thinking that if I gave them space,
I was turning my back on God.
I believed He would turn away,
that my emotions were too much
for Him to bear.

in reality,
it was in those moments of brokenness,
when I felt most distant,
that He drew closer.
it wasn't weakness; it was resilience.
when I felt weak,
God showed me how strong I was.

I've learned to speak love
where criticism once lived,
to extend grace to the parts of me
that still ache.
the way forward isn't to silence them,
but in forgiving myself
for believing them.

I wasn't born to fail,
nor shaped by the hands of lack.
the God who breathed life into me
isn't a God of poverty, nor of despair.

in His image, I am crafted.
rich in purpose,
sewn with the threads of legacy.
the world tries to tell me otherwise:
that success is reserved for the rich,
that hard work is the life of the poor.

but the truth?
the Creator lives within me,
so I am made to be fulfilled.

in the vastness of night's breath,
I know His love as my silent companion,
the confidence in stillness,
the wisdom in tranquility,
the grace to see myself
without looking away.

love met me in darkness,
not to erase it, but to hold it.
He sat beside me,
until I learned to sit with myself,
to feel the warmth of a flame
already glowing within.
no need to reach for it anymore,
I am His home,
His keeper,
His light.

I love love
for who He has made me to be,
glowing in the dark,
where I can finally see.

I thought I needed you,
but I needed God more.
His plans are not to harm,
but to prosper, and in His time,
when the soul is steady,
and the heart is full, love will come.

for now, I rest in the knowing
that my journey is guided,
my steps are ordered,
and His timing is always perfect.

I've learned that love
is the most significant power we hold.
its purpose is to connect,
to heal, to empower.
through love, we step into our roles
as co-heirs with Christ,
inheriting the ability
to bring healing to the world.

this is my calling:
to love deeply, genuinely,
so that others may see
the source of my love, Him.

love transformed me.
it killed my anger,
it taught me to forgive myself,
to love my younger self,
to tell her she isn't alone,
that death isn't the answer,
and that God's love
is waiting to heal her.

God's love was my first refuge.
He was my friend when I had none,
the one I cried to
when no one else could hear.

then, He became my lover,
revealing that He loved me first,
long before I knew His name.
it's not easy to trust Him,
especially when current struggles
overshadow the promise.
but love is the antidote,
the cure to fears.

this earth's native tongue is love.
everything responds to it;
everything is rooted in it.

with love,
the world around me shifts,
because divine love
is the most powerful tool
I have ever known.

when I think of love, I think of peace.
the light gleaming on your face
as you sit under the sun,
eyes closed, taking it all in.
love is gazing at the moon
through a window,
marveling at how the world works.

it's the feeling of looking at another,
hearing their stories,
and wanting to hug them
in a warming embrace.
love looks like Jesus, open arms,
willing to endure the cross,
to prove His love for me,
for us all.

genuine love doesn't manipulate.
doesn't pretend to gain.
it feels like patience
and looks like sacrifice.

love teaches me something new every day:
to be patient when I am angry,
to forgive when I am hurt,
to choose kindness
even when it feels undeserved.

love isn't found in control.
it doesn't demand perfection
or insist on what could be.
love begins where expectations end.
it sees the bruises and chooses to stay.

to accept someone
is to hold their truth—
the parts they offer freely
and the parts they try to hide.
it's to embrace their limitations
as places where love can make its home.

to appreciate someone is to cherish,
not what they can give you,
but all they are.

appreciation is in the simple gift
of their presence.
it's a heart posture of honoring
who they are today,
not who you hope they'll become.
it's to find joy in the act of loving,
to let them know they're seen,
they're treasured, they're loved,
just as God does.
in loving this way,
we become keepers of love.

for so long, I looked at others,
seeing pieces of my soul
in their brokenness.
I loved deeply, but without direction,
pouring into cups already cracked,
watching my love drain away,
never noticing the gaping hole in mine.

I thought love was bending backwards,
folding myself
into the shape of their needs,
silencing my cries
so theirs could ring louder.

I chased potential,
dreaming of what they could be,
blind to what they weren't.
they didn't know love,
and maybe neither did I—not yet.

then, I met Him.
a love without conditions,
without fear of rejection,
betrayal, or blindness.
a love that forgives
without keeping score,
that sees the greatest in me,
even when I saw nothing.
a love that stoops down,
just to meet me where I am.

what I hated in myself
was a reflection of His perfection,
tainted by fear, by hurt,
by misunderstanding.

I feared love because I feared myself.
the vulnerable me, the messy me,
the me who didn't think I deserved it.
but love isn't earned,
it's not a transaction.
love is, because He is.

I began to love first
the ones who scared me most:
myself, my family, my friends.
I stopped running,
stood still long enough
to see that the people I avoided
were handpicked by God
to teach me the love I feared.

I am learning
that love isn't approval-seeking,
or losing myself to gain another.
it's not deception
disguised as affection,
or sacrifice rooted in self-neglect.

love is longsuffering,
when my family tests my patience
but I express sympathy anyway.
it means calling out the action,
not condemning the person.

it's knowing that anger, fear,
or sadness can twist their words,
can drive their actions
to places they didn't mean to go.

it's meeting their outbursts
with compassion,
holding them accountable
without tearing them down.
because love isn't blind.
it sees the hurt behind the behavior,
the intention behind the flaw.

love is kind,
when I meet my reflection
with gentleness instead of shame.

love is vulnerable.
it invites trust and integrity,
even when fear whispers otherwise.
it's understanding that my past self,
the girl who manipulated, projected,
avoided, was still learning,
still healing, still worthy of love.

death hides in the stress of wanting,
in the meaning given to things
that were never meant to matter.

happiness is in what we create,
what flows from the heart,
and lives beyond us.

to be fulfilled is to live for more
than the world's narrow measures.
we were made to give, share,
love, and be loved,
to leave behind traces of meaning
that no possession could ever fathom.

there's a moment in the rush,
when faces blur into one another.
the city pulses, and for just a second,
we meet, and we remember:
each gaze holds a world,
an entire life lived in silence.
a heart beating in sync
with the noise of the streets,
a story untold,
beneath the height of the skyline.

fear tells us we're isolated,
that nothing can understand
the burden we carry,
the dreams we chase in the shadows.

but we're not so different,
as we pass each other in the streets,
invisible in plain sight.
we each hold our battles,
but in this shared space,
we're never truly alone.

love assures us
that we're not invisible in the crowd,
in the hum of the subway,
in the distant chatter of strangers.
we are seen.

when we perceive that we're all part
of this city of souls,
a metropolis built on stories,
we realize no one walks this earth
without love touching them,
without some thread of connection
binding us all.

in a city of endless possibilities,
sonder becomes the spark,
but love is the fire that heals,
the one truth that moves us
from isolation to unity,
from fear to belonging.

love isn't a static state,
it's a continuous process
of growth and evolution.
it's a journey of self-discovery,
learning to give and receive love
in its myriad forms.
it's a dance
of vulnerability and strength,
moments of profound connection
and periods of necessary solitude.

embrace the messiness of the journey,
the ups and downs,
the twists and turns
that shape your understanding of love.
let each joyful
and challenging experience
deepen your capacity
to love and be loved.

in the dishwater, I sit
greasy, chipped, and worn,
the remnants of another meal
clinging to my edges.

from here, I can see the china cabinet,
its plates gleaming like polished moons,
untouched, unchallenged
by the portions of a meal.
they're admired for their appearance,
not their purpose.

I used to long for their life,
perched high on pedestals,
safe behind glass,
never knowing the scrape of a knife,
the tension of a heavy serving.

I've learned there's wisdom
in the cracks.
those plates may shine,
but they've never felt
the scrubbing of a sponge,
the rough hands of expectation
polishing them into perfection.
they know nothing of being rinsed clean,
of shedding the residue
of a life well-lived,
of scars earned through use,
only to be used again.

my cracks tell stories.
my stains hold memories.
I've been filled, emptied,
and filled again.
each time stronger, more seasoned
by the hands that chose me.

I no longer envy the china.
they're only for display.
I was made to serve, carry,
and be part of the mess.
here in this dishwater,
I see there is beauty in being used,
in being real.

scrolling through social media,
I pass time,
though time never stands still.
each swipe reveals new goals,
new comparisons.

I heart videos, click profiles,
drawn into the glow of highlights,
a shadow lurking in their successes.
I watch their moments unfold,
wondering why mine feels stagnant.

subconsciously, I wish it were me
posting their milestones,
receiving their praise.
I start counting what I lack,
and scarcity creeps in,
a thief hiding in the algorithm.

scarcity is a curse,
and comparison is its servant.
what is it with outshining one another,
when all lights can shine as bright?
comparison dims the glow.

the only secret to shining bright
is self-acceptance.
there's enough abundance for us all.
as long as there's a candle,
it can always be lit.

some candles don't come with matches,
but there's more than one way
to make a fire.
we all carry fuel,
a spark waiting to ignite.
when we shift our focus
from what we lack to what we have,
we find the remedy to scarcity
and the grace of gratitude.

I offered my love with excitement,
every thought carried my joy,
care, and hope for connection.
later, the response came,
distant,
short,
as if I had told the best joke
that I ever thought of,
and the room just stared at me
laughing alone at my punchline.

for a moment, I felt it,
the sting of rejection,
the embarrassment creeping in.
the old me would've spiraled.
I would've dissected their words,
assigned meaning to their silence,
and told myself:
they don't care, so why should I?
this is why
we shouldn't care about anyone.

this time, I chose to let it go.
I don't know why
they responded that way.
maybe they were caught up
in their thoughts.
maybe they didn't know
how to accept love
when feeling so distant.

or maybe,
it didn't mean anything at all.
their reasons are theirs to keep.
it's not my job to dig into them,
to screw my brain
trying to decode their feelings.

what I do know is, my love was sincere.
my joy was real,
my intention was pure.
and that's enough.
it feels good to share love,
to let them know they're treasured,
to offer my care without restraint.

their response doesn't diminish
the love I give.
this is what it means to love deeply:
to hold no fear of rejection,
to know that my role is simply to love.
the rest is not my problem.

the mind is a storyteller,
crafting narratives without permission.
it weaves threads of anxiety,
writing scripts for people
who never agreed to play their part.

I thought I knew the story,
that my love was misplaced,
that my excitement
was met with indifference.
yet the truth was straightforward,
I didn't know the whole picture.

how often do we do this?
build castles of misunderstanding,
fill the buckets with assumptions,
and lock ourselves inside.
the stories we tell ourselves
are just that—stories.
they're not truth, nor are they reality.

the next time my mind begins to spin,
I'll stop and remember,
without their consent,
I can't write their thoughts.
without their words
I cannot decide their hearts.
my perceptions are interpretations,
not definitive conclusions.

even if you don't believe in Him,
He holds a truth within you, within me.
He is in all of us,
it's why we're called
to treat one another with love,
kindness, and respect.
disrespecting and dishonoring each other
dishonors Him.

I AM isn't exclusive.
it's not reserved
for the powerful or famous.
it's universal, boundless,
and free for all.

so when you say I am,
remember His name is in you.
and when you honor others,
you honor Him.

I choose life with intention.
I choose to create a path of love,
to bless God and myself,
knowing that with Him, I lack nothing.

everything I desire is already mine,
because He is my abundance.
no longer will life decide for me.
I take the reins,
walking with spirituality,
co-creation, and discipline.

with God, the barren paths will bloom,
and the impossible
will bow to the possible.
this choice I make today
is the pathway to my breakthrough.

I don't even write secrets in my diary.
can you imagine?
something meant for my eyes only,
and yet I write as if
someone might read it one day.
I fear my thoughts being exposed,
so I filter them,
twisting the truth, using codenames,
and even lying to myself.

but with Him?
I don't have to hold anything back.
I can release every thought
and every feeling
transparently without fear of judgment.
no masks, no pretense, no editing.

He is my safe space.
where I can release, let go,
and just be my imperfectly,
perfect human self.
when I ask myself,
what does God mean to me?
the answer lies
in the title of this journey:
love found me.

at my loneliest,
when I wanted to be loved
so badly it hurt,
He was the one who saw me so lovingly.
I didn't have to change myself
for Him to want me.

He gives me what I need and more,
even when I don't deserve it.
with Him, I am the main character,
admired, adored, and appreciated.
He cries for me, dies for me,
over and over again.
He bears insults for me,
and still, I've questioned Him.
ignored Him, disobeyed Him,
and mistreated Him.
yet, He never turned away.

even when I felt like
I'd lost His trust or faith in me,
He found ways
to let me know that wasn't true.
He stays.
He speaks through others to remind me
He loves me now and forever.

His love is overwhelming
in its vastness,
and feels so deeply personal.
it feels good to be loved by the Creator
of everything I adore:
the night, the moon,
the stars and sunsets.
and to know that He sees me
as more beautiful than all of it.

you could compare me
to the most breathtaking place
in the world, and still,
He would choose me.
to be honest maybe I'm a bit shallow,
but I love knowing He loves me
more than I ever could love myself.

this love humbles me,
and inspires me
to love Him more in return.
that's why I want to know Him
and for others to know Him too.

His love makes living easier,
even in a world that often feels
like falling apart.
working is traumatizing,
inflation is depressing,
and relationships are... big sigh.

despite it all,
His love remains a refuge.
His love isn't something I earned,
it's nothing I could ever lose.
in the end, love found me.

I am loved.
I am chosen.
I am His.

if we're love,
then love is how we return home.
and if love found me,
it will find you too.

anchor

anchor

whether you use them for Bible study, prayer points, or affirmations, these scriptures provide a starting point for those seeking wisdom in the Word of God, derived from the easy-to-read version (ERV). while it can't replace reading the Bible, let these verses and prayers inspire you to find strength and guidance in God's truth. Christ Himself speaks some of these scriptures, and some are spoken through the Holy Spirit; all in all, every Word in the Bible is intentional and carries a Spirit that will manifest when spoken or read. God's Word cannot be taken away from you. it has been settled even before your birth; these promises were already made, and you are waiting for them to be found. so believe in the Words you see here; they've been personally curated to bring joy, peace, comfort, grace, and the wealthiest of all, love.

love is patient and kind. love is not jealous,
it does not brag, and it is not proud. love is not
rude, it is not selfish, and it cannot be made angry
easily. love does not remember wrongs done
against it. love is never happy when others
do wrong, but it is always happy with the truth.
love never gives up on people. it never
stops trusting, never loses hope, and never quits.

God, as you said in 1 Corinthians 13:4-7,
I pray you surround me with patient and kind love. send
me love that isn't jealous, that doesn't brag, a love that
isn't proud. surround me with love that isn't rude, not
selfish, and cannot be made angry easily. may I
maintain love that doesn't remember wrongs done
against it. may I be filled with love that is never happy
when others do wrong, but it's always happy with the
truth. send me a love that'll never give up on me, a love
that'll never stop trusting me, and that'll never lose hope
or quit on me. in Jesus' name, Amen.
(1 Corinthians 13:4-7)

don't ever let love and loyalty leave you. tie them
around your neck, and write them on your heart.

*Lord, I pray that no matter who tries to hurt or change
me, please never let love and loyalty leave me. tie them
around my neck, and write them in my heart. in Jesus'
name, Amen.
(Proverbs 3:3)*

so we know the love that God has for us, and we
trust in that love. God is love. everyone who
lives in love lives in God, and God lives in them.

- 1 John 4:16

we love because God first loved us.

- 1 John 4:19

love your enemies. pray for those
who treat you badly. if you do this, you will be
children who are truly like your Father in heaven.
He lets the sun rise for all people, whether they
are good or bad. He sends rain to those who do
right and to those who do wrong. if you
only love those who love you, why should you get
a reward for that?

- Matthew 5:44-46

"I give you a new command: love each other. you
must love each other just as I loved you. all people
will know that you are My followers if you love
each other."

- John 13:34-35

"if the world hates you, remember that they hated Me first. if you belonged to the world, the world would love you as it loves its own people. but I have chosen you to be different from those in the world. so you don't belong to the world, and that is why the world hates you."

- John 15:18-19

you should owe nothing to anyone, except that you will always owe love to each other. the person who loves others has done all that the law commands.

- Romans 13:8

your love must be real. hate what is evil. do only what is good. love each other in a way that makes you feel close like brothers and sisters. and give each other more honor than you give yourself.

- Romans 12:9-10

I pray that the God who gives hope will fill you with much joy and peace as you trust in Him. then you will have more and more hope, and it will flow out of you by the power of the Holy Spirit.

- Romans 15:13

"'Love the Lord your God with all your heart, all your soul, and all your mind.' this is the first and most important command. and the second command is like the first: 'Love your neighbor as you love yourself.'"

- Matthew 22:37-39

let everyone see that you are gentle and kind. don't worry about anything, but pray and ask God for everything you need, always giving thanks for what you have.

- Philippians 4:5-6

our love should not only be words and talk. no,
our love must be real. we must show our love by
the things we do.

- 1 John 3:18

yes, I am sure that nothing can separate us from
God's love—not death, life, angels, or ruling
spirits. I am sure that nothing now, nothing in the
future, no powers, nothing above us or nothing
below us—nothing in the whole created world—
will ever be able to separate us from the love God
has shown us in Christ Jesus our Lord.

- Romans 8:38-39

do the best you can to live in peace with everyone.
My friends, don't try to punish anyone who does
wrong to you. wait for God to punish them with
His anger.

- Romans 12:18-19

why am I so sad? why am I so upset? I tell myself
"wait for God's help! you will again be able to
praise Him, your God, the One who will save you."

- Psalms 42:11

the Lord will lead you. He Himself is with you.
He will not fail you or leave you. don't worry,
don't be afraid!

- Deuteronomy 31:8

"I say this because I know the plans that I have for
you." this message is from the Lord. "I have good
plans for you. I don't plan to hurt you. I plan to
give you hope and a good future."

- Jeremiah 29:11

later, Jesus talked to the people again. He said, "I
am the light of the world. whoever follows Me
will never live in darkness. they will have the light
that gives life."

- John 8:12

most important of all, love each other deeply.
because love makes you willing to forgive many
sins.

- 1 Peter 4:8

"I have told you these things so that you can have
peace in Me. in this world you will have troubles.
but be brave! I have defeated the world!"

- John 16:33

when I am afraid, I put my trust in You. I trust
God, so I am not afraid of what people can do to
me! I praise God for His promise to me.

- Psalms 56:3-4

Christ died for us when we were unable to help
ourselves. we were living against God, but at just
the right time Christ died for us. very few people
will die to save the life of someone else, even if it
is for a good person. someone might be willing to
die for an especially good person. but Christ died
for us while we were still sinners, and by this God
showed how much He loves us.

- Romans 5:6-8

my God will use His glorious riches to give you everything you need. He will do this through Christ Jesus.

- Philippians 4:19

"I leave you peace. it is My own peace I give you. I give you peace in a different way than the world does. so don't be troubled. don't be afraid."

God, please give me peace in a different way that the world does. give me a level of peace that can't be taken away from the world, so I won't be troubled. so I won't be afraid. in Jesus' name, Amen.
(John 14:27)

I will build a great nation from you. I will bless you and make your name famous. people will use your name to bless other people. I will bless those who bless you, and I will curse those who curse you. I will use you to bless all the people on earth."

this is God's promise to Abraham, although it was made to him, we can still use it to speak over our lives. we can tap into the blessings of Abraham:

God, I humbly ask You to build a great nation from me. bless me and make my name famous, may my name be used to bless other people. bless all who bless me, and curse those who curse me. please use me to bless all the people on earth, in Jesus' name, Amen.
(Genesis 12:2)

the Spirit God gave us does not make us afraid.
His Spirit is a source of power and love and
self-control.

- 2 Timothy 1:7

we have sufferings now, but these are nothing
compared to the great glory that will be given to
us.

- Romans 8:18

always be full of joy. never stop praying. whatever
happens, always be thankful. this is how God
wants you to live in Christ Jesus.

- 1 Thessalonians 5:16-18

but the Lord said, "My grace is all you need. only when you are weak can everything be done completely by My power." so I will gladly boast about my weaknesses. then Christ's power can stay in me.

- 2 Corinthians 12:9

each one of you should give what you have decided in your heart to give. you should not give if it makes you unhappy or if you feel forced to give. God loves those who are happy to give. and God can give you more blessings than you need, and you will always have plenty of everything. you will have enough to give to every good work.

- 2 Corinthians 9:7-8

epilogue

what do you know about love? love is the most
powerful force in existence because love is God. love
is patient but never passive. it's fierce in its
gentleness and soft in its strength. it moves, builds,
heals, and transforms. love doesn't just show up
when it's easy; it shows up, especially when it's hard.
when pride says leave, love stays. when hurt says
retaliate, love forgives. love gives to someone who
may never return it the same way, because you
understand the strength it takes to love like Christ.

and then there's the other side of love—the aching,
longing, burning desire to be seen, known, and
cherished. love is a physical, spiritual, and emotional
intimacy. it's the feeling of being *undone* in some
one's presence and still being accepted. love doesn't
force itself; it's invited. love will never make you
question your worth; it reminds you of it.

love is also *pain*. it will break your heart at some
point. but it's all part of being human. people are
flawed, and the cost of loving them is knowing they
might hurt you. don't give up on love when it's
disappointing; *grieve*, *heal*, and *choose it again*. this is why
love requires grace. without it, love will not
survive.

the hardest part is that love rarely looks like what you expect. sometimes it's a slow burn. sometimes, it's someone seeing your darkest parts and choosing not to run. sometimes, it's sacrificing your pride for the sake of peace. and at times, it's releasing someone you love because keeping them means losing yourself. love will stretch you, but will also expand you. the most misunderstood thing about love is this: *you don't have to earn it.*

the world will tell you that love is a transaction, that if you look a certain way, act a certain way, and love a certain way, you will be worthy of love. but love does not operate like that. God did not love us because we were perfect. He loved us despite our imperfections. that's the standard. Jesus came as an expression of the love of God, and that's why sacrifice is the ultimate expression. the price of your healing, the price of your success, and the price of your wealth and prosperity have all been fully paid.

reader, pause with me for a moment.
notice how these words might've shifted in your mind.

how did they feel when you read them? the words about love, sacrifice, intimacy, and pain? did they make you *feel* something inside?

that's what love does. it creates a ripple effect just by existing and being spoken about. see, in these lines, I didn't just tell you about love. I invited you to experience it with me. and that's the language of love: not just to explain but to *connect*.

when I asked, "what do you know about love?" it was a question I *needed* you to answer in your heart. because love isn't just what's on the page. it's what's in your soul, what's in the space between us.

let's talk about something else for a moment. did you notice the use of italics throughout this conversation? why were those words emphasized? here's the thing about italics: they make a simple thought feel *different*. in writing, sometimes the subtle things—pauses and shifts in tone—make the biggest impact. italics can change a word's weight. it can make you feel the sentence, not just read it. when that happens, it's like a little secret being shared with you, like a little emotional nod.

when I use italics, I break the fourth wall. I'm not just talking to you on paper; I'm talking to you *in your head.* you've created a tone for me, not just *reading my words...* and that creates a new layer of connection. when words hit the soul, they don't just sit there; they *move* you.

did you feel that? when I mentioned italics, how did it change your perception of what you just read? you're not just absorbing these words; you're *experiencing* them.

in this final page, I want to reflect back to you. do you see how we're not just reading these lines but feeling them? do you feel the presence of love here?
the vulnerability, the depth, the truth?

this conversation isn't just a discussion on love, it's a *living experience.* love itself isn't static, it's fluid. it moves, breathes, and stretches. and when you're open to it, you'll become it.

you've read these words, so now, I ask you:

what do you know about love?

acknowledgments

first and most importantly, *to God, the Author of my soul,* the
One who gave me this voice, this vision, and carried me
through every page of it. none of this exists without You.

to my family, thank you for giving me something real to
write about. your love, your flaws, your complexities, they
became the ink and the lesson.

to Reverend Paul Lawson, thank you for your spiritual guidance,
for praying me through the places I didn't have strength for,
and reminding me that love must lead.

to Uncle Godfrey Crentsil, thank you for being the bridge.
it was through you that this divine connection was made.
without your alignment, the door may have never opened.

and *to my destiny helper, Mr. Frank Amo Owusu,* you saw
something in this book that I hadn't yet seen in myself. you
believed when I was unsure. you invested, not just
financially, but in the weight of my purpose. because of you,
sharing my voice with the world felt possible.

to Dr. Doyle, thank you for affirming my gift with sincerity.
your belief in my artistic expression inspired my passion
into a calling.

and *to God, again,* thank You for the people You've placed in
my life. to walk beside me, believe in me, and lift me when
I forgot how. this book is not just my story. it's the evidence
of Your love, weaved through every name, every act of grace,
and every serendipity You orchestrated.

Thank You.

i

www.ingramcontent.com/pod-product-compliance
Lightning Source LLC
Chambersburg PA
CBHW021710120626
46545CB00004B/1490